SPELLI[NG]

for
YEAR 6

2,000 WORDS
Every Child Should Know

KS2 English
Ages 10-11

STP

ABOUT THIS BOOK

Using a **fresh approach** to spellings lists, this illustrated collection of Spelling Words is designed **to make spelling fun** for your child whilst ensuring they master essential spelling rules covered by the end of Year 6.

Containing **2,000** carefully selected **level-appropriate** words, this book is made up of **70** Themed Spellings Lists that

- Have **brightly-coloured illustrated backgrounds** and **engaging titles**
- Cover **loads of topics** that **actually interest children** such as Dinosaurs, Ghosts, and TV
- Relate to other **areas covered at school** like geography, the Tudors, and recycling
- Target **key words that children overuse** (e.g. 'look', 'fast', and 'big')
- Quietly introduce **specific areas of spelling** that children need to know (e.g. using prefixes and suffixes, doubling consonants, and including silent letters)
- Are made up of **25 to 30 words each**

HOW TO USE IT

All the **lists are self-contained**, so you can work through them **in order**, or, you can dip in to use them for **focused practice**. And, as these lists are themed, they are **also a useful resource** for a range of **writing projects and exercises**.

For your convenience, an **Index** to the **spelling rules, patterns, and themed areas** dealt with by each of the lists is included at the **back of the book** on page 40.

Published by STP Books
An imprint of Swot Tots Publishing Ltd
Kemp House
152-160 City Road
London EC1V 2NX

www.swottotspublishing.com

Text, design, illustrations and layout © Swot Tots Publishing Ltd
First published 2020

Swot Tots Publishing Ltd have asserted their moral right under the Copyright, Designs and Patents Act, 1988, to be identified as the author of this work.

Typeset, cover design, and inside concept design by Swot Tots Publishing Ltd.

British Library Cataloguing-in-Publication Data. A catalogue record for this book is available from the British Library.

ISBN 978-1-912956-19-7

CONTENTS

CONTENTS Cont.

HEAD-SCRATCHERS

aural	council	metal
oral	counsel	mettle
bazaar	dual	naval
bizarre	duel	navel
boarders	eminent	sort
borders	imminent	sought
cast	foreword	suite
caste	forward	sweet
coarse	gorilla	swat
course	guerrilla	swot

Riddle Me This

baffle	enigma	perplex
bewilder	flummox	ponder
brainteaser	hint	poser
challenge	labyrinth	problematic
clue	lateral thinking	resolve
confound	maze	riddle
confuse	muse	solve
conundrum	mystery	stump
crack	mystify	unknowns
cryptic	paradox	untangle

Mamma Mia!

balcony	fresco	regatta
bandit	graffiti	riviera
broccoli	influenza	spaghetti
cappuccino	lava	stiletto
casino	magenta	tarantula
ciabatta	malaria	terracotta
confetti	manifesto	tombola
ducat	pepperoni	umbrella
espresso	propaganda	vendetta
extravaganza	quarantine	vermicelli

Im- The Impossible

imbalance	impartial	imported
immaterial	impatient	imposed
immature	imperceptible	impossible
immigrate	imperil	impractical
immobile	impersonal	imprecise
immobilise	impersonated	imprisonment
immoral	implant	improbably
immortal	implausible	improper
immovable	implode	imprudent
impaired	impolite	impure

Burnt To A Crisp

arson	combustion	kindling
ashes	embers	roasted
blackened	firebug	scalded
blaze	flame	scorching
bonfire	furnace	searing
burn	glow	simmer
cauterised	hearth	singe
char	ignite	smoulder
cinder	inferno	tinder
combustible	inflammable	wildfire

As Cold As Ice

Antarctic	frosted	icebox
Arctic	frosty	icicle
black ice	glacier	iciness
block	glittering	melting
chilliness	hail	rime
chilly	harden	rink
cracking	ice cap	skating
crystal	ice cube	solidify
freeze	iceberg	thaw
frost	icebound	tundra

Joining Forces 1

backache	earthquake	scapegoat
backbone	fireworks	sidekick
backlog	forecast	skyscraper
bedrock	forefather	slapstick
blueprint	headquarters	spearmint
brainchild	household	stronghold
carefree	keystone	sunbathe
commonplace	lifeblood	sweetmeat
commonwealth	lukewarm	wasteland
drawbridge	pinstripe	watchdog

Terrible Lizards

agile	feathered	quadruped
avian	fossil	remains
bony armour	fossilized	skeleton
carbon dating	herbivore	Triassic
carnivore	herd	vertebrate
Cretaceous	horned	
disappearance	Jurassic	
excavate	leviathan	
extinction	obliterate	
fearsome	prehistoric	

I Spy With My Little Eye

browse	glimpse	peruse
consider	inspect	regard
contemplate	investigate	review
examine	look	scrutinise
focus	monitor	seek
gape	notice	stare
gawk	observe	study
gawp	peek	survey
gaze	peep	view
glance	peer	watch

It's Not Rocket Science

analysis	empirical	objectivity
behaviour	experiment	observation
breakthrough	experimental	organisation
cause	experimentation	procedure
data	graphs	proof
demonstration	hypothesis	research
development	laboratory	scientific
discipline	measurements	structure
discovery	measuring	systematic
effect	method	theory

Mapping The World

altitude	landscape	polar
atlas	latitude	population
climate	longitude	rainfall
continent	meander	rivers
contours	metropolis	sea
equator	mountains	soil
gradient	nations	subcontinent
hemisphere	ocean	terrain
landlocked	physical features	tributary
landmass	plains	tropics

Happy Endings 1

auspicious	subconscious	pretentious
conscious	suspicious	repetitious
delicious	tenacious	scrumptious
ferocious	vicious	superstitious
gracious	voracious	vexatious
judicious	ambitious	
luscious	cautious	
malicious	fictitious	
precious	infectious	
precocious	nutritious	

Double Trouble

allergic	command	annihilate
ballerina	comment	anniversary
cellophane	commerce	antenna
collage	commit	cannibal
colleague	committee	cannon
dwelling	dilemma	colonnade
gazelle	immune	pennant
repellent	shimmer	personnel
satellite	summit	pinnacle
stallion	summon	tyranny

Lion-Hearted Or Chicken-Livered?

audacious	gutsy	faint-hearted
bold	heroic	frightened
brave	intrepid	lily-livered
courageous	plucky	petrified
daredevil	resolute	scared
daring	stout-hearted	terrified
dauntless	valiant	timorous
determined	cowardly	unheroic
fearless	craven	wimpy
gallant	dreading	yellow

Inside And Out

encased	personal	open-air
enclosed	private	outdoors
indoors	surrounded	outer
inner	walled	outermost
innermost	within	out-of-doors
interior	alfresco	outside
internal	beyond	outward
intimate	common	public
inward	exterior	surface
nuclear	external	without

In- The Incorrect

inability	incompatible	indistinct
inaccurate	incompetence	inedible
inactive	inconclusive	ineffective
inadequate	inconsiderate	inefficiency
inadvisable	inconsistency	ineligible
inanimate	inconsistent	inequality
inappropriate	incorrect	inexperience
inattentive	indefinable	infamous
inaudible	indefinite	inhumane
incapable	indirect	injustice

Silent, But Deadly

aisle	gnat	psalm
align	gnaw	rendezvous
asthma	government	salmon
beret	handkerchief	scheme
chaos	knuckle	scissors
colonel	mechanic	subtle
column	mnemonic	wrath
debris	mortgage	wrestle
depot	parliament	wriggle
glisten	plaque	yacht

LOL!!!

cackle	hilarity	smile
chortle	howl	snicker
chuckle	hysterical	snigger
crack up	jocular	snort
deride	laugh	titter
gag	mirth	
giggle	mock	
grinning	peals	
guffaw	ridicule	
hilarious	roar	

Working Out

aerobics	judo	stretch
apparatus	leotard	therapeutic
athlete	lockers	trainer
athletics	Lycra	training
biceps	massage	trampoline
endurance	membership	treadmill
exercise	metabolism	vault
fitness	muscles	weights
gymnasium	physique	workout
instructor	sauna	yoga

Happy Endings II

artificial	sacrificial	initial
beneficial	social	martial
crucial	special	palatial
especial	superficial	partial
facial	unofficial	potential
financial	celestial	residential
glacial	confidential	sequential
judicial	credential	spatial
officials	essential	tangential
provincial	influential	torrential

On Safari

breed	hunter	ranger
conservation	lodge	reserve
diurnal	nocturnal	safari
enclosure	odyssey	sanctuary
endangered	photography	savannah
excursion	poacher	solitary
exotic	predator	stalking
expedition	preservation	stampede
exploitation	prey	tracking
extinct	protection	warden

A Camping We Will Go

adventure	equipment	southern
backpack	flashlight	stove
campfire	hammock	tent
campsite	hiking	trekking
canoe	northern	undergrowth
caravan	orientation	walking
clambering	pitch	western
climbing	scenic	wilderness
compass	shelter	wildlife
eastern	sleeping bag	woodland

That Doesn't Look Right

accompany	disappear	physical
according	embarrass	prejudice
address	guarantee	queue
available	individual	restaurant
calendar	interrupted	secretary
community	medicine	separate
competition	necessary	strength
correspond	neighbour	temperature
desperate	ordinary	vegetable
determination	particular	vehicle

Greased Lightning

abruptly	galloping	snappily
accelerating	hastening	speedily
apace	hastily	sprightly
breakneck	lively	swiftly
briskly	post-haste	tearing
careering	promptly	
dashing	quickly	
energetically	rapidly	
fleeting	rattling	
flying	rushing	

A Snail's Pace

crawling	languid	sluggish
creeping	leisurely	straggling
dawdling	lingering	tardy
deliberate	loitering	trailing
drifting	measured	unhurried
easing	plodding	
gradual	ponderous	
haltingly	shuffling	
inching	slothful	
lagging	slow-moving	

Il- The Illegible &
Ir- The Irresponsible

illegal	irredeemable	irresponsibly
illegality	irregular	irretrievable
illegally	irregularity	irreverence
illegible	irrelevance	irreverent
illegitimate	irrelevant	irreversible
illiteracy	irreparable	
illiterate	irreplaceable	
illogical	irresistible	
irrational	irresistibly	
irreconcilable	irresponsible	

The Root Of The Matter I

antebellum	autobiography	circumference
antechamber	autocorrect	circumflex
antedate	autograph	circumnavigate
antemeridian	automate	circumscribe
anteroom	automatic	circumvent
aquamarine	automobiles	
aquaplane	autonomous	
aquarium	autonomy	
aquatic	autopilot	
autobiographies	autosave	

Mother Tongue

accent	idiolect	regular
articulate	idiom	rhetoric
bilingual	informal	slang
communication	jargon	speech
diacritic	linguistic	style
dialect	multilingual	syllable
diction	phonetic	syntax
fluency	polyglot	translation
formal	pronunciation	vernacular
grammar	proverbial	vocabulary

Native Speakers

Arabic	Hungarian	Portuguese
Bengali	Indonesian	Russian
Chinese	Italian	Spanish
Czech	Japanese	Swedish
Danish	Korean	Thai
Dutch	Mandarin Chinese	Tibetan
English	Norwegian	Turkish
French	Pashto	Urdu
Greek	Persian	Vietnamese
Hindi	Polish	Yoruba

Happy Endings 111

achievable	deniable	questionable
adorable	enviable	recommendable
answerable	favourable	regrettable
applicable	imaginable	respectable
appreciable	knowledgeable	supposable
attachable	likeable	tolerable
breathable	mentionable	uncountable
changeable	persuadable	understandable
consumable	preventable	unforgettable
debatable	programmable	unreachable

Tuck In!

bolt	glut	stuff
breakfast	gorge	sup
chew	graze	swallow
consume	gulp	swig
cram	guzzle	swill
devour	have	
dine	munch	
eat	overeat	
feast on	quaff	
feed	relish	

Spicing Things Up

allspice	fennel	vanilla
anise	fenugreek	condiments
caraway	ginger	flavouring
cardamom	juniper berries	powdered
cayenne pepper	mustard seeds	seasoning
chilli pepper	nutmeg	
cinnamon	paprika	
cloves	peppercorns	
coriander seeds	saffron	
cumin	turmeric	

Sage, Rosemary & Thyme

aloe vera	fennel	sage
basil	ginkgo	sorrel
bay leaves	lavender	tarragon
catnip	lemon grass	thyme
chamomile	marjoram	herbaceous
chervil	mint	
chickweed	nettle	
chives	oregano	
coriander	parsley	
dill	rosemary	

BOUQUETS OF FLOWERS

armada	convoy	stack
bouquet	fleet	string
bunch	fusillade	suit
bundle	library	suite
cache	pack	tuft
chest	quiver	
clump	ream	
cluster	set	
clutch	sheaf	
collection	squadron	

D Is For Danger

adverse	hazardous	powder keg
chancy	hostile	precarious
cliffhanger	insecure	precipice
dangerous	jeopardy	risk
deadly	knife-edge	riskiness
dicey	lethal	threat
fatal	menacing	tinderbox
flashpoint	minefield	uncertain
hairy	peril	unsafe
hazard	perilous	unstable

What Was That Noise?

apparition	headless	souls
aura	illusion	spectral
bodiless	incorporeal	spectre
bogey	phantasm	spirit
creepy	phantom	spook
ectoplasm	poltergeist	spooky
eerie	revenant	sprite
ghostly	scary	vision
ghoul	séance	wight
haunted	shadowy	wraith

ABRACADABRA!

abracadabra	familiar	sorceress
beldam	foretell	sorcery
black magic	hag	spell
broomstick	hex	voodoo
chant	hocus-pocus	warlock
charm	jinx	white magic
conjuror	magician	witch
crone	magus	witchcraft
curse	predict	wizard
enchantress	sorcerer	wizardry

And Then...And Then...

additionally	initially	secondly
altogether	lastly	specifically
conversely	likewise	thirdly
equally	moreover	unlike
fifthly	nonetheless	whereas
finally	notably	
firstly	obviously	
fourthly	overall	
including	particularly	
indeed	regardless	

When In Rome...

accelerate	cordial	hostility
agriculture	corollary	lagoon
ambiguous	culinary	lateral
animate	culpable	linear
astute	deity	lucrative
aviation	dulcet	luxury
benefactor	duration	medium
centurion	endorse	peninsula
commentary	equestrian	privilege
condone	exasperate	procure

True Or False?

artless	simple	devious
blunt	sincere	double-dealing
candid	straight	false
direct	straightforward	hypocritical
forthright	truthful	insincere
frank	cheating	lying
honest	crafty	sly
open	cunning	sneaky
outspoken	deceitful	treacherous
plain	deceptive	untruthful

Happy Endings IV

accessible	divisible	legible
admissible	edible	permissible
audible	eligible	plausible
collapsible	flexible	possible
collectible	forcible	reprehensible
compatible	inadmissible	reversible
constructible	indivisible	suggestible
credible	intangible	susceptible
deducible	invincible	tangible
destructible	invisible	visible

Save The Planet

biodegradable	ecosystem	non-renewable
biodiversity	emissions	ozone layer
biohazard	environmentalist	pollution
climate change	extermination	preserve
compostable	fallout	renewable
contaminate	fauna	surroundings
decimation	flora	sustainable
deforestation	global warming	toxic waste
desertification	greenhouse effect	unrenewable
eco-friendly	greenhouse gases	unsustainable

GOING GREEN

biowaste
cardboard
compost
convert
decompose
discarded
disposal
environmental
fertilizers
garbage

incineration
kerbside
landfill
organic
packaging
plastic
recycle
reprocess
repurpose
rubbish

sorting
sustainability
toxicity
trash
treatment

Near And Far

adjacent
adjoining
alongside
around
attached
beside
central
close
handy
immediate

local
nearby
neighbouring
next-door
together
afar
apart
distant
extreme
faraway

far-flung
farthest
furthest
inaccessible
isolated
lonely
outlying
outmost
remote
removed

ALL AT SEA

anchor	harbour	paddle
astern	launch	porthole
bows	league	prow
buoy	lifeboat	rescue
cabin	lighthouse	rigging
coastal	mainsail	rudder
coastguard	mooring	seabed
cruise	nautical	tiller
disembark	oar	voyage
fathom	offshore	wheel

All Aboard!

berth	freight	shunt
buffer	guard	sleeper
cargo	high-speed	station
carriage	inspector	ticket
commuter	intercity	timetable
diesel	locomotive	track
driver	mainline	transit
electric	monorail	transportation
engine	passenger	tunnel
express	railway	underground

Grrrrrr!

aggravate	harass	rankle
anger	incense	ruffle
annoy	infuriate	tease
antagonise	irk	trouble
bother	irritate	vex
displease	madden	
disturb	nag	
enrage	pester	
gall	plague	
goad	provoke	

As Big As An Elephant

astronomical	extensive	prodigious
behemoth	gigantic	sizeable
bulky	huge	spacious
bumper	humungous	substantial
cavernous	immense	titanic
colossal	infinite	towering
considerable	juggernaut	tremendous
cumbersome	large	vast
elephantine	massive	voluminous
enormous	outsize	whopping

ON THE SMALL SIDE

bite-sized	mini	small
cramped	miniature	teensy
diminutive	minuscule	teeny
dinky	minute	tiny
fractional	modest	undersized
insubstantial	negligible	
itsy-bitsy	petite	
Lilliputian	pocket	
limited	pocket-sized	
little	poky	

Oodles Of Ologies

anthropology	meteorology	sociology
archaeology	methodology	technology
astrology	microbiology	terminology
biology	nanotechnology	theology
chronology	neurology	zoology
cosmology	palaeontology	
criminology	pharmacology	
etymology	physiology	
geology	psychology	
ideology	radiology	

Happy Endings V

abundance
alliance
allowance
annoyance
arrogance
assistance
assurance
brilliance
clearance
defiance

distance
elegance
entrance
fragrance
grievance
guidance
hesitance
hindrance
ignorance
instance

insurance
nuisance
observance
radiance
relevance
reliance
substance
surveillance
tolerance
vengeance

TUTANKHAMEN & CO.

ankh
artefacts
bureaucracy
cataract
civilization
delta
discoveries
dynasties
empire
excavation

flooding
hieroglyphics
irrigation
kingdom
lapis lazuli
mastaba
mummification
obelisks
papyrus
pharaoh

pyramids
reliefs
rituals
ruins
sarcophagus
scribe
silt
sphinx
unification
worshipping

As Cool As A Cucumber

calm	placid	undismayed
collected	poised	unemotional
comfortable	relaxed	unexcited
composed	sedate	unfazed
cool	self-possessed	unflustered
easy-going	serene	unmoved
level	settled	unperturbed
mellow	tranquil	unruffled
nonchalant	unbothered	untroubled
peaceful	unconcerned	unworried

On Edge

agitated	edgy	shaky
alarmed	flustered	tense
anxious	fretful	troubled
apprehensive	jittery	twitchy
bothered	jumpy	uncomfortable
concerned	nervous	uneasy
disconcerted	panicked	unnerved
dismayed	perturbed	unsettled
distracted	ruffled	uptight
disturbed	shaken	worried

A Is for Amazing

amazing	great	spectacular
astounding	incredible	staggering
awesome	inspirational	stupendous
breathtaking	lovely	sublime
brilliant	magnificent	super
excellent	marvellous	superb
fabulous	outstanding	terrific
fantastic	phenomenal	uplifting
glorious	remarkable	wicked
gorgeous	sensational	wonderful

The Root Of The Matter 11

hyperactive	microcosm	polyester
hypercompetitive	microdot	polygon
hypercritical	microfibre	polygraph
hyperlink	microfilm	polymath
hypersensitive	micromanage	polythene
hypertext	micro-organism	
hyperventilate	microphone	
macrocosm	microscopic	
microchip	microsurgery	
microcomputer	microwave	

Both Sides Of The Coin 1

careful	trusty	thoughtless
conscientious	unfailing	unconscientious
dependable	careless	undependable
reliable	heedless	unreliable
responsible	ill-considered	untrustworthy
sensible	inconstant	
sound	neglectful	
steady	negligent	
thoughtful	rash	
trustworthy	reckless	

THE TUDORS

accession	factions	rebellion
Catholics	favourites	Reformation
circumnavigation	intrigue	reign
clergy	maritime	Renaissance
controversy	marriage	royal house
dissolution	monarchy	sovereignty
divorce	monasteries	succession
Elizabethan	persecution	taxation
executions	plot	uprising
expansion	Protestants	warring

Happy Endings VI

absence	existence	pretence
audience	influence	prudence
correspondence	innocence	reference
defence	insolence	residence
dependence	lenience	resilience
difference	licence	science
disobedience	obedience	sentence
eloquence	offence	sequence
essence	patience	silence
evidence	presence	violence

What Are You Feeling?

admiration	euphoria	misery
agitation	gratitude	nervousness
anxiety	grief	pain
boredom	guilt	pleasure
despair	happiness	pride
disappointment	heartache	regret
disbelief	homesickness	sadness
embarrassment	jealousy	surprise
enjoyment	joy	wonder
envy	merriment	worry

Both Sides Of The Coin II

efficient	chaotic	rumpled
methodical	cluttered	scruffy
neat	dishevelled	shabby
ordered	disorderly	unkempt
orderly	disorganised	untidy
organized	inefficient	
shipshape	jumbled	
spruce	messy	
tidy	muddled	
uncluttered	ramshackle	

And The Orchestra Played...

arpeggios	harmony	scales
bar	libretto	sheet music
baton	melody	solo
brass	notation	soloist
choir	octet	sonata
classical	opera	stave
clef	orchestral	strings
composer	percussion	symphony
conductor	quartet	treble clef
conservatoire	rehearsal	woodwind

Music To My Ears

accordion	guitar	recorder
bagpipes	harp	saxophone
banjo	keyboard	sitar
bassoon	lute	tambourine
castanets	lyre	timpani
cello	mandolin	trombone
clarinet	oboe	trumpet
double bass	organ	tuba
flute	piano	viola
French horn	piccolo	violin

Joining Forces II

big-hearted	heavy-handed	long-lasting
bow-legged	high-class	long-lost
broken-down	high-definition	short-lived
broken-hearted	high-end	short-tempered
four-by-four	high-octane	short-term
hard-and-fast	ice-cold	thick-skinned
hard-boiled	light-headed	thin-skinned
hard-earned	light-hearted	tight-fisted
hard-headed	long-awaited	tight-fitting
heavy-duty	long-haul	tight-lipped

Binge-Watching

broadcast	episode	programme
buffering	film	ratings
bulletin	footage	reality TV
channel	live	screen
chat show	miniseries	season
commercial	newscaster	sitcom
docudrama	newsflash	streaming
documentary	phone-in	terrestrial
downloading	pilot	update
drama	presenter	viewer

Greeks Bearing Gifts

academy	catastrophe	ethic
aesthetic	ceramic	eucalyptus
agony	chrome	galaxy
ambrosia	chrysalis	gastric
amphibian	cyan	hypodermic
antidote	demographic	nostalgia
architect	diagram	orthodox
arctic	energetic	parallel
aristocracy	epoch	problem
cardiac	ether	symbol

Are These Clean Or Dirty?

clean	unblemished	grubby
cleansed	unpolluted	mucky
hygienic	unsoiled	muddy
laundered	unstained	polluted
pure	washed	soiled
purified	blemished	stained
sanitary	contaminated	unclean
spotless	filthy	unhygienic
sterile	greasy	unpurified
sterilised	grimy	unwashed

Chillaxing!

absorbing	enthusiast	pursuit
activity	escapism	recreation
amateur	fascinating	relaxation
amusement	game	satisfying
collecting	hobbies	sport
craze	indulgence	
creative	interest	
distraction	leisure	
diversion	obsession	
enjoyable	pastime	

V Is For Vile

alarming	grim	nightmarish
appalling	gruesome	outrageous
atrocious	harrowing	shocking
blood-curdling	hideous	spine-chilling
dire	horrendous	terrible
distressing	horrible	terrifying
dreadful	horrid	tragic
fearful	horrific	unpleasant
frightful	horrifying	unspeakable
ghastly	nasty	vile

ZZZZZZ...

asleep	insomnia	shuteye
catnapping	late night	siesta
daydream	lie-down	sleepwalking
doze	nap	sleepyhead
dreamless	nightmare	slumber
drift	nod off	snooze
drowse	oversleep	snore
drowsy	power nap	undisturbed
forty winks	repose	wakeful
hibernate	rest	weariness

INDEX

In the following entries, the letter 'A' refers to the upper list on the page, while 'B' refers to the lower one.